The
KNOWN
Personal Branding
Workbook

MARK W. SCHAEFER

ISBN-13: 978-1542401814

ISBN-10: 154240181X

INTRODUCTION

This workbook is meant to accompany the book *KNOWN* by Mark W. Schaefer. *KNOWN* is available through most online retail channels.

The *KNOWN Personal Branding Workbook* provides additional prompts and exercises to help you develop an actionable plan to become known in the digital world.

Table of Contents

I GETTING TO WORK

I'm excited that you're on the path to becoming known!

The best way to use this workbook is as an accompanying piece to the book *KNOWN*, either upon completion of the book or as you read through each chapter.

The first two chapters of *KNOWN* are dedicated to setting the stage. Why is this work important? And can anybody become known?

Main themes of the Introduction and Chapter 1 include:

- The source of influence today is not necessarily tied to your title, your position on an organizational chart, or the awards you've won. Today, you must build an equity of influence by becoming known.

- Being known can provide a sustained and permanent career advantage over those who are not known in your industry.

- "Known" is not the same as famous. It's not about having millions of fans and red carpet appearances. Being known is about approaching your web presence with an intent that creates the proper authority, reputation, and audience to realize your potential and achieve your goals … whatever they might be.

- Becoming known takes more than following a dream or passion. It requires a plan to give you the best possible chance of success.

- Becoming known is an evolutionary process. You don't have to be an expert in something to ultimately succeed as long as you embrace a mindset of continuous and urgent learning.

- The case studies in the book demonstrate that everyone has the chance to be known today. Many of the people in the book rose from obscurity and even poverty to become successful.

- Some national cultures discourage people from standing out. However, in many professions, the world is flat and we compete on a global scale. You have almost no hope of competing in a global marketplace unless you're known.

- Case studies in the book demonstrate that people of different nationalities, personality types, and ages can all become known.

EXERCISE 1.0
WHY DO YOU WANT TO BECOME KNOWN?

There are many great reasons for becoming known. Some people want to:

- Write a book
- Launch a speaking career
- Become a consultant
- Be named to a prestigious board
- Remain relevant in their field for years
- Attract donations for a charity
- Sell digital products online
- Run for political office
- Achieve recognition for work
- Earn a college teaching position
- Build a brand to build a business
- Become a paid "influencer"
- Open more doors in order to attract more sales
- Be in a position for a promotion
- Publish in an industry journal
- Share their passion and ideas

Think about what you want your life to be two years from now. In the space below, write your thoughts on why you want to become known. What advantages would this create for you?

I want to be known so I can …

2 FINDING YOUR SUSTAINABLE INTEREST

Chapter 1 concludes with a summary of the four-step path outlined in the following chapters:

- **Step One: Finding your place.** You must be known for SOMETHING. What is your unique voice, your distinctive place, your *sustainable interest* on the web?
- **Step Two: Finding your space.** Occupy a large enough space to make a difference.
- **Step Three: Finding your fuel.** Content is the fuel for building a personal brand today.
- **Step Four: Creating an actionable audience.** Your network is your net worth. How do you connect to the audience in your space in a way that is actionable and helps you achieve your goals?

Chapters 2 and 3 launch the first step on the path to becoming known by helping you define your sustainable interest.

Becoming known must involve more than mere passion. Sometimes a hobby is just a hobby. Perhaps the most important factor is endurance. A sustainable interest is something that you love. It's a topic you'll have fun with for years to come, but it's also a theme you want to be known for, something that will help you achieve your long-term life goals. In this section you'll go through several exercises to define your sustainable interest. You don't have to complete all of these exercises, but try at least two or three that resonate with you.

People who are able to endure and work for years to stand out typically have a sustainable interest that connects to the well-being of others. Having a greater purpose behind your sustainable interest provides the glorious reward for all your hard work.

Without purpose, many will find it impossible to maintain an idea for months, for years, for a lifetime. For some, a sense of purpose dawns early, but for others, the motivation to serve becomes clear only after you get a response and feel the love from your new audience.

Let's start this section by focusing on purpose.

EXERCISE 2.1
SENSE OF PURPOSE

Do you have a sense of purpose behind why you want to become known? Think about what you want to be known for – how does that connect to other people? How does it benefit others? If you can't answer that now, don't worry. It may come later. But if you have a strong sense of purpose, write about that below because it will certainly be part of your sustainable interest.

Becoming known will connect me to people and help them in these ways …

EXERCISE 2.2
THE "ONLY I ..."

Can you finish this sentence: Only I ...

Are you the most experienced, the most caring, the smartest, the most entertaining, the most trustworthy? Are you the best at service, at explaining things, at creating new approaches and ideas? Are you unique because of your education, the perspective that comes from where you live, who you know, or what you do? Why do your friends love you? What is it about you that keeps them coming back to your circle year after year?

Another clue to zeroing in on your "Only I" statement is the sort of questions people ask when they come to you for advice. Maybe this is a sign of what you're really known for.

Ask for feedback from colleagues, co-workers, and customers who observe you in your workplace now. What is the "elevator pitch" for you?

ONLY I ...

EXERCISE 2.3
THE 2 X 2

A highly effective way to determine your distinct place on the web is to actually visualize it. Can you find an underserved audience that matches your sustainable interest?

If you're familiar with your industry, you can probably name two distinctive characteristics of the audience you would most like to reach, like wealth, education, age, and activity levels.

Create a simple 2 X 2 chart like the one in the *KNOWN* book with those two characteristics, and then plot where your competitors might fall:

EXERCISE 2.4
THE CORE VALUES MASH-UP

The book describes this exercise as the opportunity to combine a topic (like food, fitness, or leadership) with a core value. This is a good way to find a new angle, even in a crowded niche. Circle some of the values below that represent aspects of your personality, and then add them to your topic. The goal is to create something that is new but also very exciting for you. And you don't have to stop here. Add other values that are also important to you.

Peace	Influence	Honesty
Wisdom	Happiness	Fairness
Status	Truth	Athletic/Fitness
Family	Kindness	Humor
Fame	Spirituality	Stylish
Wealth	Loyalty	Frugal
Power	Environment	Luxury
Authenticity	Trust	Craftsmanship
Joy	Knowledge	Charity
Success	Reliability	Building
Integrity	Teamwork	Independence
Love	Competitiveness	Design
Friendship	Commitment	Education
Justice	Creativity	Scientific

Here are some examples of how people featured in *KNOWN* combined a value and a topic to create something new:

- Fanny Slater combined food with her background in comedy to make funny blog posts.
- Aaron Lee merged his short stature with a love of fashion to become known for providing fashion tips for short men.
- Pete Matthew joined his expertise in wealth management with spirituality to create a financial podcast meant to lift people up and inspire them.
- Isadora Becker loves food and movies, so she started a cooking YouTube channel featuring famous recipes from the movies and TV.
- Jennifer James combined her love of blogging with her passion for social justice to become known for uniting bloggers for social causes.

Combine your interest with values you circled above and write a few ideas here:

EXERCISE 2.5
STRENGTHS FINDER

This exercise will require the outlay of a few dollars, but it's worth it.

The Gallup Company developed a simple and inexpensive online quiz called the Strengths Finder Test. More than 14 million people have taken this test, and for good reason – it's a remarkably accurate personality assessment! You can find this test at www.gallupstrengthscenter.com.

The Strengths Finder Test may be the fastest and most accurate way to determine your sustainable interest. Often the answer is right in front of us but we're so close to … ourselves, I suppose … that it's difficult to see how we shine in the world.

Take this test and then reflect on the results. Pay attention to your emotional response when you read the results. Which characteristics created a strong response? That could be a powerful clue to your purpose and sustainable interest.

- **Do the results reveal my "Only I?"**
- **Can my strengths be combined with a topic of interest to help me stand out?**
- **Was there an "a-ha moment" that sheds light on my core values?**

EXERCISE 2.6
THE TENNIS BALL

KNOWN contains a series of questions generated from work by author Warren Berger. Answering these questions may help you define your sustainable interest. The first question is, "What's your tennis ball?"

The most successful people are obsessed with solving an important problem, something that matters to them. They're like a dog chasing a tennis ball with energy and determination. To increase your chances of success, you must find your "tennis ball" – the thing that pulls you.

What am I obsessed with?

EXERCISE 2.7
WHAT ARE YOU DOING WHEN YOU FEEL MOST ALIVE?

What's the time and place when you feel most alive – whether it's when you're solving a problem, creating, connecting with someone, traveling, teaching, learning, or doing something else? What is a sustainable interest that will allow you to do more of this?

What makes me come alive? Here are the places and activities that ignite my passions:

EXERCISE 2.8
WHAT IS SOMETHING YOU BELIEVE THAT ALMOST NOBODY AGREES WITH?

This question from PayPal cofounder Peter Thiel is designed to help you figure out what you care about, and determine whether it's worth pursuing. It can be tough to find an idea or belief that isn't shared by many others. Originality is deceptively difficult!

But if you can find a problem or challenge that no one else is tackling, it may be a place where you can sculpt your own niche and create value. You don't want to be interchangeable with your competition.

What view of the world seems to be unique to me?

EXERCISE 2.9
WHAT ARE YOU WILLING TO TRY NOW?

One of the best ways to find your sustainable interest is through experimentation. Most people try to discover their purpose by reading books or taking self-help classes. But the "a-ha moment" may never come unless you actually try something through temporary assignments and moonlighting.

Am I in a position to test my sustainable interest? Name a few ways to do this:

EXERCISE 2.10
WHAT IS YOUR SENTENCE?

This question helps you distill your sustainable interest to its essence by formulating a single sentence that sums up who you are and what you aim to achieve. A leader with a clear and strong purpose can be summed up in a single line. Here's "The Sentence" for a few famous people:

- Mahatma Gandhi: "I am the father of passive resistance to create social change."
- Abraham Lincoln: "I freed the slaves."
- Charles Darwin: "I developed a theory of evolution to explain biological differences."

What would your sentence be? If your sentence is a goal not yet achieved, then how will your sustainable interest help you get there?

Here are some ideas for "my sentence:"

EXERCISE 2.11
VISUALIZE YOUR FUTURE

Relax for a moment. Imagine yourself two years in the future. You're being interviewed for a podcast. What questions are you being asked?

Stay in the future visualization. You're about to speak to a group of your peers at an industry conference or local club. You're so excited to share your ideas! What is your speech about?

One more time. Your friends tell you that you should write a book because you're so helpful and knowledgeable. What would your book be about?

I am being interviewed about:

My speech topic would be:

I might write a book about:

EXERCISE 2.12
35 HEADLINES

Think about the content you might create about your sustainable interest that will establish your authority and connect to an audience. Are you thinking about blogging? Videos? A podcast?

Now make a list of the first 35 topics you'll cover about your idea. No need to get into details — just write down the headlines. For your content ideas, you might want to answer people's questions, provide your take on industry issues, and tell stories about relevant lessons from your career.

This exercise will provide two insights. First, it delivers a perspective on how easily this topic will be to sustain. Second, this exercise helps you refine your interest. People who complete this list have no trouble with the first 10 topics. But when you get to the last 10 ideas, it requires deep thought. Look at the entire list. Is the theme consistent? When you get to the end, does your topic change at all?

1 _____

2 _____

3 _____

4 _____

5 _____

6 _____

7 _____

8 _____

9 _____

10 _____

11 _____

12 _____

13 _____

14 _____

15 _____

16 _____

17 _____

18 _____

19 _____

20 _____

21 _____

22 _____

23 _____

24 _____

25 _____

26 _____

27 _____

28 _____

29 _____

30 _____

31 _____

32 _____

33 _____

34 _____

35 _____

EXERCISE 2.13
SUMMARIZING YOUR SUSTAINABLE INTEREST

Let's take an important step by summarizing your sustainable interest. Look through your responses to your Section 2 exercises. Do you see a theme emerging that points to a topic that is:

- Aligned with your strengths
- Providing purpose because it benefits others
- About a distinctive topic that helps you reach your goals
- Inexhaustibly fascinating to you

Here are examples of effective sustainable interest statements from some of the people featured in the *KNOWN* book:

- Shawn Van Dyke: "I leverage my construction industry experience and love for teaching by helping other professionals solve their business problems."
- Antonio Centeno: "I feel strongly that your appearance can help build your self-image and self-confidence. I want to share this with others and help them succeed through helpful short videos."
- Neale Godfrey: "I serve as the financial voice for Baby Boomers, millennials, and their offspring. I want families to take control of their financial future."

This is an important statement for you to create, but if you're still stuck, don't panic! There are other exercises in this book to help refine your thinking about ways to stand out.

Do your best at this point to articulate your own sustainable interest statement, recognizing that you may never truly know your place until you've been working through the process for a period of time.

Chances are you won't precisely identify your sustainable interest on the first try. But you're never going to move ahead and improve unless you *begin*.

Here is my sustainable interest statement:

3 DETERMINING YOUR SPACE

In the quest to become known, finding your sustainable interest simply isn't enough if you can't present it in a channel that captures the attention of an audience big enough to make a difference. To succeed, you must have the perfect intersection of *place* and *space*.

In the last section, I helped you find your ideal *place,* or what you want to be known for, and beginning with *KNOWN* Chapter 4 you'll spend some time with this careful decision of *space.* Even if you're passionate, dedicated, and committed to the task ahead, your effort will end in frustration if the competition is so severe that you're never discovered or heard.

Failing to find a meaningful, uncontested space is the primary reason people fail in their effort to become known.

To give yourself the best chance to succeed, you need to determine:

- Is your niche big enough to matter?

- Is it oversaturated already?

- Are there people who will be attracted to your sustainable interest?

The first priority is to examine the competition for your sustainable interest. Have you found an uncontested niche, is the competition moderate, or is there so much competition that you need to revisit your topic?

The first two exercises in this section will help you define the competition (the supply) you're likely to encounter for your topic. The third exercise will determine the "demand" for your topic. The ideal situation is to occupy a space with low supply and high demand. The last exercise focuses on ways to carve out a workable space even if you're working an exceedingly crowded topic like food or fitness.

EXERCISE 3.1
DETERMINING THE SATURATION IN YOUR NICHE

Chapter 4 starts with a story about Dr. Jamie Goode, whose success emerged, in part, by being among the first in his niche of wine blogging. He admits that his achievements would not be so assured if he started today (there are *thousands* of wine bloggers now!).

Certainly this would be the ideal situation – being the person to pioneer a new segment. And there are still lots of opportunities for you. The internet is just beginning. Most of the ideas that will dominate our lives 10 or 15 years from now haven't been invented yet. There's still a chance for you to get in on the ground floor of *something*.

To begin this analysis, we must do a simple test to judge the information density of your space.

If you have an idea of what you want to be known for – your sustainable interest – Google it. Think of some of the key terms that are associated with your identity and look at the search results. How much competition do you have?

- If your search returns fewer than 500,000 results, this is extremely good news. You could be a true pioneer in this space.

- If the search returns between 500,000 and 1 million results, well … you still might be able find success using some of the techniques in the next chapter. But it's going to require patience and work.

- If the search exceeds 1 million results, that's a pretty saturated niche you're pursuing. You'll need to tweak it a bit or find a new angle on how you're thinking about your sustainable interest.

As you conduct your search, also pay attention to see if anyone "owns" the space – even if it's crowded. For example, a search on the topic of "succession planning," returns more than 9 million entries. However, there was no single person writing about this subject. There were many articles on this topic but the top search results showed that nobody owned it. Even with millions of results, this is a wide-open space.

What is the initial result of your search? Are you in a position to pioneer a new space, or does it make sense to tweak your sustainable interest?

EXERCISE 3.2
ADVANCED SEARCH TECHNIQUES

Perhaps you don't aspire to be known worldwide. Maybe you want to be known for your views on training and development in Poland, for example. In this case, you'll need to refine your analysis.

This is an optional process called the Keyword Optimization Index (KOI) contributed by Roy Ishak, an award-winning copywriter and SEO specialist from The Netherlands:

- Step 1: Use the Keyword Planner of Google AdWords or another keyword suggestion tool to determine the search volume of your focus keywords.

- Step 2: Find out how much competition you have by Googling: *allintitle:keyword* (the keyword would be something related to your sustainable interest).

- Step 3: Divide the search volume (the size of your market from the Keyword Planner) by the amount of "allintitle" search results (your competition), and multiply that number by the search volume again. For example:

> **Search volume:** 100,000 results
> **Search results (competition):** 2,000,000 results
> **Formula:** $(100,000 \div 2,000,000) \times 100,000 = 5,000$

Do this test for a variety of keywords to determine which ones are the most popular and have the least competition, regardless of the population of a country. The higher the resulting number, the higher your chance to rank well in the organic search results of Google and the higher your chance of succeeding in this market.

If you're trying to dominate a niche in a specific region of the world, narrow your investigation by country:

- To adjust **search volume,** every keyword suggestion tool has an option to "select country." For example, if you select "The Netherlands," the tool shows search volumes of Holland.

- For the **competition factor,** every person around the globe uses their own national version of Google. People in America use google.com. Citizens in the Netherlands would use google.nl, in France it would be google.fr, and so on. When you use *allintitle:keyword,* filter in the version of Google for a certain country so that Google displays the competition you would be facing for results in that country.

EXERCISE 3.3
GOOGLE TRENDS ANALYSIS

The dream scenario is to discover an uncontested niche with growing interest from your potential audience. This is easily determined by turning to Google Trends.

Take the same keywords you used in the first exercise in this section and insert them into a free site called Google Trends. The result will be a useful trend line of search volume over the years. An upward trend means there is growing demand for your ideas. If you're considering several different sustainable interests, you can plot them on the same chart for comparison.

Unfortunately, Google only provides a relative indication of the size of the audience. The trend line does not provide an absolute view of the number of people searching for those terms.

Are more or fewer people becoming interested in my sustainable interest?

EXERCISE 3.4
COMPETITIVE ANALYSIS

Chapter 5 in *KNOWN* goes through opportunities to distinguish yourself through a *space*, even in a crowded niche. Some of the ideas include:

- Develop a unique content tone or point of view.
- Move to a new social platform within your niche.
- Dominate a content type.
- Pioneer a new content form.
- Differentiate through frequency.
- Appeal to a new demographic target or region.
- Leverage relationships with influencers.
- Curate content.

To fully understand how you might stand out in your space, you'll have to look around your marketplace and do a small competitive analysis. Read the case studies and examples in Chapter 5 carefully so you understand these potential points of differentiation, and then visit competitor sites to understand where they fit into the information eco-system of your industry.

Use the table on the following page as a way to organize your notes on competitor activities.

As you conduct your competitive analysis, keep in mind that some of the factors on this table could be part of the 2 X 2 exercise (Exercise 2.3 in this workbook). This might help you visualize open opportunities to distinguish yourself through your content.

COMPETITIVE ANALYSIS

Potential point of differentiation	Competitor 1	Competitor 2	Competitor 3
What is the competitor's tone or pont of view? How would I be different?			
What social platforms do they use? Is there an opening for me?			
What is the dominant content type? (hygiene, hub, hero)			
What is the dominant content form? (written, video, audio, etc.)			
How often do they publish? Could I establish a space through publishing frequency?			
What demographic niche do competitors appeal to? Is there an open audience for me?			
Do my competitors have relationships with industry influencers or could I somehow partner with competitors to become known?			
Are any of these competitors curating content or could that be a niche for me?			

EXERCISE 3.5
CLAIMING YOUR SPACE

At this point in Section 3 you've assessed the information density in your proposed niche to determine if your space is uncontested or competitive. You've also looked at the competition to discern whether there is some opening in *how* your message can be presented that might be unique.

Now it's time to take a shot at naming your space. Where is the spot that is just for you in the information eco-system of your field?

Here are examples from the book of how people succeeded by claiming just the right space:

- James Altucher found his space in the crowded field of self-help blogging through his *tone*.
- John Lee Dumas carved a niche by supplying helpful advice on his podcast every day. His differentiator was *frequency*.
- Suzy Trotta stands out from realtors in her region by using *social media platforms* in a unique way.
- Dr. Jamie Goode established his space in the wine blogging field by being an *early mover*.
- Neale Godfrey recognized that nobody was publishing books that helped families learn about money. She fought to establish her space through drive and persistence. Like Dr. Goode, she found an *uncontested niche*.

Now it's time to claim your space.

My plan to become known requires that I establish my sustainable interest in this space:

4 CREATING A CONTENT PLAN

To have an opportunity for real authority on the web and vast reach, you need a certain type of content that has the depth and breadth to be discoverable. To become known, you need to focus on one of these four types of "rich" content:

- **Written content like a blog:** Blogs are easy and low-cost to start but can be time-consuming to maintain. They're a primary contributor to search engine ranking success and an excellent way to build thought leadership and community.

- **Audio content like a podcast:** A podcast is an internet-based radio show. Anyone can start their own program today. A study by Edison Research showed that podcast listeners are more loyal, better educated, and wealthier than other online audiences. The cost of maintaining a podcast can be moderate to high, depending on frequency.

- **A video series:** This content type is excellent when you need to entertain, demonstrate, and teach. Engagement levels can be high, and video is especially popular with younger audiences. The cost and complexity of producing videos for YouTube can vary widely from live streaming to complex productions.

- **Visual content:** Infographics, illustrations, and photographs are ideal if you're building an audience on Facebook, Instagram, or Pinterest. They attract a lot of social-sharing and typically can be produced at a reasonable cost.

Only high-quality, conversational content from at least one of these sources will provide the fuel you need to stand out and become known. Which one is right for you? The following exercises will help define this for you.

EXERCISE 4.1
CONTENT COMPETITIVE ANALYSIS

Revisit competitor sites and look for evidence of a blog, podcast, YouTube channel, or Instagram account. Fill out this table, noting whether they seem to have a dominant presence in any of these content areas.

There is another measure on this table which may be unfamiliar to you – *site authority,* also known as *domain authority.*

Domain authority may be a critical consideration in deciding the type of content you produce and finding where your competitors may be vulnerable. Domain authority is an indicator of how strong a website's "pull" is in the eyes of Google. A site with high authority will have an advantage in terms of the traffic it will pull from web searches.

I have some bad news and some good news. The bad news is that Google won't tell us that domain authority number. The good news is that a company called MOZ has a tool that will allow you to at least estimate your number for both you and your competitors. You can find this tool at https://moz.com/researchtools/ose.

Domain authority is a score (on a 100-point scale) developed by MOZ that predicts how well a website will rank on search engines. Use domain authority when comparing one site to another or tracking the "strength" of your website over time.

To determine domain authority, MOZ employs machine learning against Google's algorithm to best model how search engine results are generated. Over 40 signals are included in this calculation. Because there are so many variables, your score may vary over time, so you might want to check on this at least once a quarter.

Nevertheless, domain authority provides a good indicator of how you rank against competitors. If you have a domain authority score higher than your competitors, it's a great opportunity for you to pull away, especially with a focus on blogging. If a competitor has a score much higher than you, it's probably because they're already creating a lot of great content.

If all the scores in your analysis are low – say, below 30 points – this is an indicator that you can use content to build authority over time.

A complete analysis of domain authority is impossible to provide here, but there is plenty of information on this measurement – and how to improve it – on the MOZ site.

Content Competitive Analysis

Potential point of differentiation	Competitor 1	Competitor 2	Competitor 3
Is there a blog? Is it being updated regularly? Is there engagement?			
Does the competitor host an active podcast?			
Does the competitor have a YouTube channel? Do they post regularly?			
Does the competitor have an Instagram account? Is it active?			
What is the site authority of these sites, according to the MOZ calculator?			

EXERCISE 4.2
CONTENT AND PERSONALITY TYPE

Exercise 4.1 should only provide *guidance* on what kind of content you need to produce. Sure, you want to find a distinctive path, but at the end of the day, you must enjoy what you're doing.

Perhaps this is an easy decision. If you like to write, then write and ignore what the competitors are doing. If you're fascinated by video or podcasting, give that a try. It's most important to enjoy what you're doing because you may spend years doing it.

If you're trying to decide what to do, consider your personality type and how that might fit with a certain content type. Between the slow, cerebral demands of blogging and the in-the-moment improv of Snapchat is a continuum of content options for the range of human personalities. Here's an overview of how content might match with personality.

FOR EXTROVERTS	FOR INTROVERTS
Snapchat	Blogging
Live-streaming video	Writing books/audiobooks
Product reviews	Recorded webinars
Online courses	Newsletters
Twitter chats	Comics and cartoons
Live video chats	Visual content/photography
Live speaking events	Presentations posted to SlideShare
Podcasts on your own	Podcasts where you interview others
Solo videos	Videos where you interview guests

By thinking through *what* you publish and *where* you publish it, you can create a plan that's most likely to fit your personality. I want to emphasize that I'm not trying to pigeonhole people. We are diverse and lovely as we are. There's absolutely no reason why a shy person can't enjoy posting on Snapchat and a chatty person wouldn't love stirring things up on a blog. These lists simply provide some food for thought. If you're unsure of what might be the best fit for you, experiment with a few different platforms and discover the ones you love.

What content form do you think you would love?
Which content form seems sustainable for years?

EXERCISE 4.3
THE DISCIPLINE OF CREATING CONTENT

You don't necessarily have to be an expert in anything to become known over time. Nobody starts as an expert. But you do need to have an urgency to learn, improve, and create content consistently, usually over a period of years. To become known you need to adopt a mindset of vicious consistency and continuous improvement. You need a plan.

There are three activities you need to build into your weekly routine: continuous learning, constant idea creation, and sacred time for creating content. Think this through, answer the following questions, and commit to developing your own culture of content discipline.

1. To become known, I must be a reliable authority. This doesn't have to happen all at once, but I must set aside time for reading and learning. What time during the week can I do this?

2. To become known, I must be constantly gathering ideas for my content. I am bombarded by ideas all day long. What method can I use to record ideas that come to me throughout the day through the media, questions I'm asked, and other sources of inspiration?

3. To become known, I need to commit to creating content consistently, ideally once a week. To do this I need to set aside quiet time each week to think and create. I commit to scheduling the following time on my calendar each week as if it were an important meeting.

EXERCISE 4.4
CLAMING YOUR CONTENT

I hope these exercises have helped you think through your content options. It's most important to choose something you love and, a close second, a form that is unique in your field.

Your plan to become known requires you to choose one form of rich content (written, video, audio, or visual) and establish an audience for a minimum of one year before changing or diversifying.

My preferred content form is:

5 ESTABLISHING AN AUDIENCE

Nothing makes the process of becoming known more gratifying than the moment you realize somebody out there is listening. In fact, the value of your content is zero unless somebody views it. So, the final step in your process to become known is finding your fans, the theme of Chapter 7.

When it comes to building an audience, Elsie Larson, one of the sisters behind the website "A Beautiful Mess," reflects a unifying sentiment of everyone I interviewed for this book.

"I built a readership over the course of many years," Elsie said. "I focused on quality posts that take a lot of time to write and develop, being consistent (I've been posting almost every day for several years), and being myself. The blog evolves as I evolve; it's slow and steady. Nothing happened overnight. I have never paid a penny to advertise 'A Beautiful Mess;' I just kept doing my best and a readership developed over the years. It's the product of hard work, constant evaluation, and lots of love."

These themes should be familiar to you by now. Quality. Consistency. A unique and authentic "place." Hard work.

Chapter 7 in *KNOWN* covers some of the most popular methods to attract people to your content (and keep them there), including:

- **Passive connection** through SEO, social media, promotion, and other bloggers
- **Active connection** through engagement, networking, and influencers

Most people use a combination of both methods. The following exercises will help you determine a balance that feels right to you.

EXERCISE 5.1
ESTABLISHING AN AUDIENCE GOAL

It's a good idea to set a preliminary goal. How big of an audience do you need to achieve your objectives?

One of the primary messages in *KNOWN* is that audience size does not necessarily equate to influence and power. How big of an audience is right for you?

Here are example audience sizes of some of the people featured in the book:

- Antonio Centeno, video fashion tips: 750,000 YouTube subscribers

- Tom Fishburne, business cartoonist: Tens of thousands of newsletter subscribers

- Lindsey Kirchoff, college student seeking a job: About 500 LinkedIn connections

- Dr. Alice Ackerman, pediatrician: Fewer than 25 blog subscribers

These people are successful in their unique ways and are known in their respective fields, but the size and location of the audiences they need to succeed varies wildly. The lesson here is that there's no universal answer to the question, "How big does my audience need to be?" It depends on who you need to connect with and what you want to achieve.

Life is a long path, and you meet a lot of different people along the way. Maybe all you need is one follower if it's someone who will change the course of your life.

Visualize what success would look like for you two years from today. How big of an audience do you need to achieve that success? If you have a very specific goal, like being hired by a certain company, you might even be able to identify your ideal audience by name!

To achieve my goals, my ideal audience size in two years' time would be:

EXERCISE 5.2
ESTABLISHING AN AUDIENCE-BUILDING PLAN

Chapter 7 of *KNOWN* goes into detail about different audience-building techniques, and Chapter 10 suggests that you spend a minimum of five hours per week on activities to help you become known:

- At least three hours per week creating your preferred type of content
- One hour per week igniting your content through promotion and distribution
- At least one hour per week to engage with your audience and influencers

If you want to build a large audience in a short period, it will require more time than this. The table on the next page provides an outline of a potential one-year plan for audience-building based on size. There's no cookie-cutter solution that fits every person, every industry, every goal. Choose a plan that feels right to you, and begin experimenting to see which techniques work best.

Every audience-building activity needs a blend of:

- SEO
- Paid promotion
- Relations with influencers
- Networking
- Audience engagement
- Social media

However, based on your goals and the amount of time you have, you'll need to prioritize.

Primary activities based on size of audience goals

	Small audience (less than 1,000)	Medium audience (1,000 - 10,000)	Large audience (More than 10,000)
	1.5 hours per week	2.5 hours per week	3.5 hours per week
Month 1	Networking + Social media	Networking + Social media	Networking + Social media
Month 2	Networking + Social media	Networking + Social media	Networking + Social media
Month 3	Networking + Social media	Social media + Bloggers	SEO
Month 4	Networking + Social media	Social media + Bloggers	SEO
Month 5	Networking + Social media	Audience engagement	SEO
Month 6	Networking + Social media	Audience engagement	SEO, Influencers, Promotion
Month 7	Networking + Social media	SEO	SEO, Influencers, Promotion
Month 8	Audience engagement	SEO	SEO, Influencers, Promotion
Month 9	Audience engagement	Influencers	SEO, Influencers, Promotion
Month 10	Audience engagement	Influencers	SEO, Influencers, Promotion
Month 11	Audience engagement	Influencers, Paid promotion	SEO, Influencers, Promotion
Month 12	Audience engagement	Influencers, Paid promotion	SEO, Influencers, Promotion

**Provided my audience-building goals, what plan seems best for me to try?
How aggressive do I need to be?**

6 SUMMARIZING YOUR PLAN

Congratulations on all the great work you've completed to create a personal plan to become known. Let's summarize some of the milestones on one page, and this will be your starting point.

This is my sustainable interest (Exercise 2.13):

This is the space where I will deliver my message (Exercise 3.5):

This is the one type of rich content I will create on a consistent basis (Exercise 4.4):

To build an audience, I will first focus on these activities (Exercise 5.2):

7 CONSISTENCY AND GRIT

The case studies in KNOWN emphasize the importance of vicious consistency and resilience. In her seminal book *Grit*, Angela Duckworth describes four core personality traits of people with the exceptional persistence needed to become known:

- **Love of the work**
- **Capacity to practice**
- **Purpose**
- **Hope**

How gritty are you? What is your innate ability to persist? Here's a free online test to assess your grit. Enter this code in your browser: **bit.ly/grit-test**

8 TRACKING YOUR PROGRESS

Chapter 10 in the *KNOWN* book provides a method to track your progress by tallying indicators of a growing awareness for your personal brand. These indicators might include:

- An increase in the number of visitors to your site
- A growing number of people in your online audience
- A rise in the number of inquiries, including interviews, requests for comment or content, and paid assignments

To help you track your progress, I've created an easy-to-use Excel spreadsheet exclusively for this workbook. You can access this spreadsheet and download it to your computer for free by entering this code in your web browser: **bit.ly/brand-dashboard**

ABOUT THE AUTHOR

Mark W. Schaefer is a globally recognized speaker, educator, business consultant, and author who blogs at {grow} – one of the top marketing blogs in the world.

Mark has worked in global sales, PR, and marketing positions for more than 30 years and now provides consulting services as Executive Director of U.S.-based Schaefer Marketing Solutions. He specializes in social media training, marketing strategy, digital transformation, and personal branding. Clients include both start-ups and global brands such as Microsoft, Johnson & Johnson, Adidas, and the U.S. Air Force.

He has advanced degrees in marketing and organizational development and is a faculty member of the graduate studies program at Rutgers University. A career highlight was studying under Peter Drucker while pursuing his MBA.

Mark is the author of five other best-selling books: *Social Media Explained, Return On Influence, Born to Blog, The Content Code,* and *The Tao of Twitter,* the best-selling book on Twitter in the world. You can find his podcast, The Marketing Companion, on iTunes.

He is among the world's most recognized social media authorities and has been a keynote speaker at many conferences around the world including Social Media Week London, National Economic Development Association, the Institute for International and European Affairs, and Word of Mouth Marketing Summit Tokyo.

Stay connected with Mark at www.BusinessesGROW.com and by following his adventures on Twitter: @markwschaefer.